THE SAME AMOUNT OF INK

Susan Berlin

GLASS LYRE PRESS

Copyright © 2016 Susan Berlin

Paperback ISBN: 978-1-941783-27-6

All rights reserved: except for the purpose of quoting brief passages for review, no part of this book may be reproduced or transmitted in any form or by any means, electronic or mechanical, including photocopying, recording, or by any information storage and retrieval system, without permission in writing from the publisher.

Cover art: Painting (oil on canvas) by Robert Warsager
             Photograph of painting by Tom Lauria
Author Photo: Jason Berlin
Design & layout: Steven Asmussen
Copyediting: Linda E. Kim

Glass Lyre Press, LLC
P.O. Box 2693
Glenview, IL 60026
www.GlassLyrePress.com

Acknowledgments

Grateful acknowledgement is made to the editors of the publications in which the following poems have appeared or are forthcoming, sometimes in earlier versions or under other titles:

Alaska Quarterly Review: "Settling"

Asheville Poetry Review: "No Time to Burn"

Atlanta Review: "The Elastic's Gone Out of the Rubber Band," "Vanishing Point at the Inlet," "Request Denied"

Cape Cod Poetry Review: "Many Happy Returns," "Great Grandpa Scheckter's Sound Effects"

Controlled Burn: "Broken Words"

Eye Dialect: "From My Window"

Georgetown Review: "Blue by Default"

Gimlet Eye: "Before the Party"

Harbor Stage Company Playbill: "Big Happy"

Harvard Review: "The Ferry in August"

Iodine Poetry Journal: "On This Filthy February Morning"

Mudfish: "False Witness," *"You Shouldn't Have,"* "Today, Again," "Through the Funnel of a Loose Fist"

Naugatuck River Review: "At the Thrift Shop, Christmas Eve"

New Millennium Writings: "Mistress," "Before the Ground Turns Hard"

Oberon: "Day of Atonement," "Prayer," "Shutter"

Pirene's Fountain: "Non-Stop Scarlet," "Praise for the Corpse Flower," "Unbareable Heat"

Ploughshares: "Fat Crow Above Me," "Still Life on Brick Steps"

South Road: "Richer for Its Absence," "Apples on South Road," "The Armoire"

Word Soup Poetry Journal: "The Upside of Numb"

Personal Acknowledgments

A huge debt of gratitude to my teachers — Jean Valentine, Suzanne Gardinier, Gerald Stern, Stephen Dobyns, Heather McHugh, Billy Collins, Ellen Bryant Voigt, Deborah Digges — and especially to Thomas Lux for the steadfast faith as well as the 'nuts and bolts.'

Great thanks to friends who shared their knowledge and insight: Jennifer Wallace, Robert Fanning, Gwendolen Gross, Pat Rosal, Anne Marie Macari, Jeet Thayil, Curtis Bauer, Greta Neunder, Walter Aikens, the members of the Bass River Revisionists (my smart and generous writers' group) — too numerous to list here but all deserving. And to my close readers over the years — Ross Gay, Vince Cioffi and Barry Sternlieb, whose words have guided and inspired me. And, of course, to Ami Kaye, Steve Asmussen, and the dedicated staff of Glass Lyre Press for bringing this book to its final form.

I would like to thank my brother who, instead of giving me another pair of wool gloves for my 12th birthday, gave me an LP of Dylan Thomas reading "A Child's Christmas in Wales" to which I listened over and over — face-down on the living room rug, forehead resting on crossed arms — as snow whirled outside and I fell in love with the music words can make.

To my mother in whose bottom dresser drawer I found, after her death, a bundle wrapped in yellowed newspaper and tied tight with twine, filled with clippings of poems she'd written and had published in newspapers when she was young — of which she'd never spoken.

And most of all, always, to my sons, who know my soul and have nurtured it in every possible way since the day(s) they were born. I am deeply and forever grateful.

Contents

Acknowledgments   3
Personal Acknowledgments   5

Foreword by Thomas Lux   15

One

Today, Again   19
The Armoire   20
False Witness   21
Before the Party   22
Broken Words   23
Stepping Out   24
Great-Grandpa Scheckter's Sound Effects   25
Blowing Redemption   26
You Shouldn't Have   27
In The Red   28
Still Life on Brick Steps   29

Two

Many Happy Returns	33
Comforters	34
The Ferry in August	35
Slow Dawn	36
No Time to Burn	37
Blue by Default	38
Apples on South Road	39
Negative Capability	40
Seven Storms	41
At the Thrift Shop, Christmas Eve	42

Three

The Upside of Numb	47
Beyond Dispute	48
Intermittent Hiss	49
Fat Crow Above Me	51
Performance Art	52
Startle Reflex	53
The Sun at Its Widest Point	54

Three (con't.)

From My Window	55
Incipient Ice	56
Through the Funnel of a Loose Fist	57
Breaking News	58
Before the Ground Turns Hard	59
The Elastic's Gone Out of the Rubber Band	60

Four

After Years of Forced Heat	63
Floored	64
Mistress	65
Waves and Light	66
Absent Without Leave	68
All Holy	69
Absolution on the Ferry	70
Richer for Its Absence	71
Prayer	72
Non-Stop Scarlet	73
Settling	74
Shutter	75
Praise for the Corpse Flower	76

Five

Request Denied	79
On This Filthy February Morning	80
That Date	81
Unbareable Heat	82
Big Happy	83
Peekskill Possibilities	85
Ellipsis	87
Boilerplate	88
Day of Atonement	89
Gifts from a Crow	90
Vanishing Point at the Inlet	92
About the Author	95

*For my mother, who taught me how to love,
and my sons, who taught me how to live.*

We turn, and turn, like leafy plants
to the sun of our circumstance…

— J. Allyn Rosser

Foreword
by Thomas Lux

I've been waiting a long time for this book. I mean an actual book, in print, on pages, between covers. I've been reading Susan Berlin's poems for many years — from across a table, sitting on a bench, in an office, in literary journals, etc. So: I've known how good she is, and now, with this collection, a lot more people will know that, too.

Her poems, first of all, are unflinching. She's a "deep noticer." Her poems are direct but always subtle, loaded in their detail, which is where the poetry of poetry often resides. (Wallace Stevens called it "The poetry of the thing.") I've always loved a poem in this book called "Still Life on Brick Steps." The scene is simple (it's only 15 lines): a father is leaving his wife and two children. He's in his car, driving away. The children, outside on the front porch steps — their backs to their mother watching from the window — wave goodbye to their father: "…the day our father left // for good, with hands held low, close / to our chests, so our mother / at the window behind us // couldn't see." The tension in the sadness of that moment is implicit in the desire not to hurt the mother but also to please the father. Does the father glance back as he pulls away? I doubt it. Sometimes children are put in such untenable positions and, sometimes, decades later, they make true art out of them.

These poems can also be very funny. Often at the speaker's expense. The poem with the splendidly reverberant title, "Through the Funnel of a Loose Fist," ends, after a fight with a spouse, this way: "She fills the kettle / with little more than half an inch / and, while waiting for it to whistle, // transfers the cashews he loves / from the leaf-shaped dish / into a tightly lidded jar." We (of the human species) employ different means to resist tyranny, and we can be ingenious in our pettiness.

This book is filled with images, like the above, that are more than images, that are, in fact, metaphors. (Metaphor: one of the disappearing — it seems to me — yet most sacred reasons for poetry's being. And simile, as well. It's not easy to put a new angle on the auditory part of an egg about to hatch — unless you do it before the first chirp: "…a soft ripping sound, delicate, /

a kind of slow pulling apart…" (from "Slow Dawn"). The hint in that "slow pulling apart" again suggests more than its literal intention. Particularly when the reader learns the nest and eggs were never (the speaker believed they were) there.

The poem "Many Happy Returns" describes the painting a husband was given by his mother as a wedding gift. He insists on hanging it in his and his wife's bedroom. The wife hates it because there's "Not a bird nor bud on a single broken branch. / Red grass, red sky." He's always fussing with it, adjusting it because of its skewed perspective. At one point, he takes it down, and you think, for only a moment, maybe he's removing it, maybe even to please his wife. He's not. In a blink, and set up with a line break, the poem turns chilling. "…[H]e eases it // off the hook that's good for up to 50 lbs., / placing the thing face down on the bed / to tighten, by hand, the wire." So much happens and is evoked with a minimum of prolixity and fuss. Sometimes metaphor can only be explained by metaphor.

What runs through all of these poems, though they never toot their own horns, is a huge and generous spirit. And the love it articulates. I've read many moving poems, elegies about deceased loved ones, but few have ever made me love someone else's mother as much as I love Susan Berlin's!

Of course, we never met, except in poems. There is pain and loss in these poems and never a peep of self-pity. The subjects are universal: we all experience pain (as well as joy) and losses — yet very few of us are also able to write poems as smart, and true, and insightful, and as brilliant as these.

Thomas Lux
Atlanta, July 2016

ONE

Today, Again

On the subway, a tap on my shoulder: it's
Frances Gugliotta, from 7th grade. Same curly hair,
same friendly smile with thirty years etched on.
We take turns — she screaming updates
into my ear, then I into hers — competing

with the squawking brakes, our bodies torqueing
with each turn, jerking forward and falling back
through decades of who married whom and how many kids,
who's bald, who got fat, divorced, arrested, dead.
Then Frances asks about my mother, calling her

Mrs. Warsager the way she did, and suddenly
I'm twelve, in the yellow kitchen of our house,
my mother washing dishes at the double sink
and me, drying. Frannie's in the doorway
in her pink corduroy coat, a hopeless stack
of homework and books in the crook of each arm.

She almost misses her stop. For the rest of the ride,
I try to name what it was that made me float. More than
something familiar amidst everything strange,
more than the headlines and bits of news I'll lose
between changing trains. Across the aisle, an old

poster with a black-and-white photograph asks:
Have You Seen This Missing Person? And the word
comes to me as gratitude for the unexpected
gift — the solid sound of something good but gone,
today, again, on someone's lips.

The Armoire

My parents kept getting bigger
houses as if more space would allow them
to hate each other less. The last place
we lived, my father left my mother alone
in the master bedroom and moved himself
into the spare. Nothing treasured there —

a tired cot, a vinyl ottoman with one
short leg — but the antique armoire and what
it stored: white linens and bed sheets,
hand-stitched, and, along the borders,
red tulips embroidered with light
green leaves. These, he lugged

to the basement, dumped them on the bag
of lime used for killing weeds. Once, when
the need to know what he held sacred
made my mother enter his room, she approached
the armoire and slowly opened its arched
gothic doors: on nothing, nothing inside

but emptied bottles of men's cologne
and a wall calendar not meant for any nail,
the square of each day of each month
crossed out by a thick black X,
including the month they were in
and half of the next.

False Witness

There must have been some good in him,
but all I remember is our father calling every
now and then to say he's getting married

again and would Bobby and I care to come.
True, there was that one time he spent the entire
day with us, those pictures he took:

the front of the bus with its grimy promise
of Coney Island; the green mildewed boats
that moved slow enough to go around

only once; Bobby and me in pea-coats, collars up
against the off-season gusts, back-dropped by various
games of chance. There's that shot with our heads

cocked at the same strained angle, our lips
puckered like fish, pulling at the cotton candy's
sticky mass. And then

all the exposures he took — the remainder
of the roll — of rides we didn't get to go on,
restaurants where we didn't eat.

Before the Party

On the other side of the bedroom wall
their daughter sits, pencil-straight,
at the edge of her bed so as not
to put a single wrinkle in her

starched, pleated party dress.
With each blow, she smoothes
the bedspread beside her, smoothes
her skirt over skinned knees, smoothes

her pony-tail from the rubber band
down to the bottom (likes the way
the end of it curls around her wrist
like a dog's tongue) and she sits,

ankles pressed together in ruffled
white socks and good red shoes.
When it's done, a window is raised,
a nose is blown. The girl slowly inhales,

folds her hands in her lap,
watches the door.

Broken Words

My grandfather claimed to be fluent in nine languages
but only spoke to me, poorly, in one.

He read, though, in the original tongue
from books he kept when all else was left behind,

their bindings cracked, paper flaking like Austrian pastry —
whole phrases breaking off and floating to the floor

as he turned the page. Between index finger
and thumb, he'd pick up the piece, pinched like a dead

butterfly, and slip it at random back in the book.
Soon, he couldn't remember what went where, so

he'd improvise, filling in the gaps as he saw fit,
editing Nietzsche and Goethe to agree with *him*.

When, in time, my grandmother's legs failed,
this man who had never lifted a grocery bag

carried her from bed to chair like a child, his entire spine
outlined through the back of his thin cotton shirt.

And later, when she could no longer speak and no one knew
if she could still comprehend, he'd read aloud to fill

the air with sound. Standing bedside, he'd rest
the book on the metal rail like a priest at the lectern,

each paragraph a prayer, every page another psalm,
reading till he was parched and the words sat

stillborn on his tongue. Only then did he take
the bookmark, place it in her upturned palm.

STEPPING OUT

The salesman licks a drop of mustard from one knuckle,
transfers his sandwich to the other hand to pull out a box,
chuck it onto a chair. Red shoes — the ones I've visited
each day for a week, on the way home from school.

Even the soles shine! Seven years old, and I've seen
The Wizard of Oz six times. On the balls of my feet, I swivel
sharply this way and that, standing before the slanted mirror
that shows me only from the ankles down.

These are the feet of someone whose father never left,
whose clothes were bought expressly for her and not
her older, thinner cousin. The feet of a girl who goes places,
like Sandy Sussman on Sundays in the front seat of their car.

The salesman coughs, signaling it's time for me to step out.
Hooking one finger inside the heel of each shoe, he slaps them
into the box, taps it back into the waiting slot. That night,
my mother at the kitchen table, writing letters

instead of checks to send out with the bills — her eyeglasses off
and pushed away on the vinyl tablecloth, magnifying purple grapes
to plums — she looks up and smiles, the way she only smiles
at me, and I know those shoes are mine, for the asking.

Great-Grandpa Scheckter's Sound Effects

I never saw the man
alive, although he occupied
the back room of my grandparents'
second-floor flat for several months before
he died — too sick for visitors,
especially us kids.

It was my grandmother who tended him,
measured his medicine, pulled the covers up
to what I imagined was his white-whiskered chin,
opening the door just wide enough for her
slight frame to slip in. I'd try to steal
a glimpse but he was buried
beneath the hand-embroidered quilts,
ensconced in that weird metal bed
that curled over itself at either end
like a Russian sled.

Whenever the old man turned or kicked off
the sheets, a loud "gong" would reverberate,
echoing down the hall of that railroad flat
like an engineer calling out the last stop.
My grandmother would put down her tea
precipitously — the fragile porcelain cup smacking
against the saucer — and race down the hall
to disappear into his room.

What was it she tried to keep from us?
The odor of illness, the notion of death? What
we couldn't see, we feared. Grandma, we never saw
his face, but we saw yours, and we could hear.

Blowing Redemption

When I was ten

I asked my father who was

smoking a cigarette
on the back steps

if he

        loved
          my mother.

He said
No.

So I asked him then if he had   ever

        loved
          my mother.

Taking a long drag
on his cigarette

he exhaled   a halo
the color of   regret
    above my head

and said

I don't

                remember.

You Shouldn't Have

My mother bought herself
a present once, wrapped and hid it,
as my father bid her to, between the mower

and the long-nosed can of gasoline.
She must have thought ten times and hard
before buying the gift and the Mother's Day card,

before stashing them in the detached garage
with a ballpoint pen so that, when my father returned
from his latest tryst, he could scribble his name

and print both of ours. That Sunday, as she tore off
the foiled paper and tried, for our sake, to act
surprised, how she must have hated him —

and, judging from the choice, herself, too:
a scratchy brown scarf with matching gloves,
and her favorite color, blue.

In The Red

Holding open the door like *El Cordobes*,
my father coaxes my brother to take the wheel
of the two-toned Olds he's just sold him.

Drive around the block, get the feel of it,
he says, accepting the thick roll of dollar bills
as payment down. Between them I sit, a pebble

wedged in the forked trunk of a tree. My brother's legs,
twice the length of mine, force him to slide the seat back,
far as it goes. After adjusting the mirrors, hands locked

at 10 and 2 o'clock, he scans the incandescent dials,
shifts into gear and drives, slow as a requiem mass,
down South Fullerton Ave. and, just before we pass

Mrs. Sanborn's lopsided red shack where squirrel traps
rattle on the roof from the day's catch, the odometer
flips all five nines to a line of zeroes

like mouths of quintuplets, hungry. Howling.

Still Life on Brick Steps

My brother and I without coats
on the front porch steps waved
good-bye, the day our father left

for good, with hands held low, close
to our chests, so our mother
at the window behind us

couldn't see. She stayed
inside, and when his car
took the corner, we turned

and saw her — the curtains,
long and white, parted by
her hands — her face

the face of a bride
abandoned too late, too
late, two lifetimes ago.

Two

Many Happy Returns

The husband sees nothing
wrong with it, the painting presented
to him as a wedding gift from his mother.

He claims to like the piece despite
the skewed perspective, the roof
impossibly attached to the barn.

Blunt, chopped strokes and everything
bright red. Red trees, all trunk and no leaves.
Short, jabbed lines meant to define the bark.
Not a bird nor bud on a single broken branch.
Red grass, red sky.

As for that viscous pool in the middle — a reservoir
of some kind, filled with ominous squiggles?
His mother's initials, metastasized.

Tonight, the wife lowers her book, watches her husband
lumber out of bed, tilt for the 100th time
the heavy gilt frame a quarter-inch up on the right,
step back to adjust it again — this time a bit
higher on the left — before he eases it

off the hook that's good for up to 50 lbs.,
placing the thing face down on the bed
to tighten, by hand, the wire.

Comforters

I think of my mother, trapped
in her rose-budded room during her final

but favorite season, afloat in a sea
of pillows to ease the pain, the night-table

covered with prayers in the shape of
a dozen amber bottles bearing her name,

and of how the white down comforter covered
her legs — twigs beneath the snow — and how I ran

into her room looking for my son, the school bus
having already beeped, twice; how I found her

sitting up, one knuckle pressed hard against her lips,
her comforter turned crimson from

as many leaves as my son could gather and hold,
a raucous mass of them spread across her bed

as if blown there by the wind, how she mouthed
Thank you to him as he grabbed his books,

ran past us and bounded for the door — her eyes
dazzled by the gift, lips bloodless at the thought.

The Ferry in August

It's August, and even the seagulls
are sated. A gaggle of women — sisters
of some sort — press their bellies to the railing
and bend from the waist, flailing
pastel arms in the air, bearing food.
C'mon! Take it! they implore,
a line of stage mothers begging
their children to perform.

Too hot to bake, I take
refuge in the boat's belly
where it's dark and wet,
near an open porthole, square.
Close to the water.
Inside the salt lick.

Behind schedule, the ferry flies.
The white strip of sand on the shore
runs by sideways (a lover
in a train station
saying good-bye) and

I squint as the sun glints
off the water like my mother's
glasses at the beach while,

outside, Cheez Doodles rain,
then float, tiny orange boats
atop an already salty sea.

Slow Dawn

The long distance argument
left me an audience of one
for the fog-horn's late-night solo.

Sleep, what little there was,
left no mark and now, still half-in that
unkept dream, I hear the shooshing
of Sunday rain, the best kind — once over
easy, tuck the shoulder under the quilt —

when from inside a tree — probably
the scrub oak whose branches in summer
scratch the rusty screen — a ruffling of wings,
a bird coming home and leaving again,
each absence longer than the one before,

and then, a soft ripping sound, delicate,
a kind of slow pulling apart like the shell
being peeled from a hard-boiled egg,

and soon the tentative chirp of newborn birds
at dawn. Before daylight floods the room,
I run shoeless outside, to see. No birds, no tree.
Nothing scratching at the glass but me.

No Time to Burn

Buffered, horizontally, by boughs
of a thousand pines, the wind
comes to me in these rented woods
filtered, like a tune my uncle hummed

through his moustache.
Summer birds, disturbed at night,
squawk like squatters chased
from a fire they've built

but won't have time to burn. I know
this lullaby: the trees moan it
when a storm's about to hit. I hold
my pillow like a raft, in advance.

Blue by Default

Above the book's edge, I see a man
at the high end of middle age combing through
the sand as if he's lost something small.

Grey and long, his hair levitates at half-mast
when he nears the water, stoops to cup both hands,
scoop up some foam and smoothe it over his freckled dome,
down to the fly-blown ends.

That's when he seems to sense me there
and straightens his spine, tucks both thumbs
into the waist of his trunks and pivots to approach —
a seagull with stubby legs, in search of lunch.

I'm compelled, but not by him. What's clear
is the woman moving toward me through no volition
of her own. A woman mute by design, tattooed on his chest
in eternal discomfort, nude and perched in heels so high
they defy engineering. And her eyes — unable to return

the gaze of the man who enslaved her. Eyes like decals,
dull as chronic pain. Blue by default but flatter than that,
faded down from the once brilliant black.

Apples on South Road

For once, the black horse close enough
to the fieldstone wall to touch.

I leave the car in neutral and approach.
Standing to the side, I stroke his mane, brush back
the fly-away hair from his jack-of-diamond eyes
and, again and again, watch it fall.

The horse keeps nudging my shoulder, my arm,
as if starved, as if stroking were the last thing he needs,
so I leave to rush home — ten minutes of slow winding road —

to grab some apples from the bowl. What makes me
polish the skins before peeling them, then take time
to cut the pieces smaller and smaller, careful
to remove the seeds, the starry cores, I don't know,

but when I return, the horse has turned away,
his regal head dipping from one bucket to another
on the field's fallow side. Nothing makes him notice me.
So I stand and wait with my plastic bag as the air grows chill
and the day's light turns dim, slowly eating

the apples I washed and polished, cut and cored
and brought, I thought, for him.

Negative Capability

This is how you've chosen to live — like your mother,
who asked nothing from this world
and did not subscribe to the other.

She was content with a closetful
of cooking smocks and her one good dress.
She, without hope: blessed.

Seven Storms

Barns are collapsing under the weight of wet snow,
fractured rafters crashing onto the backs of startled cattle.

Seven storms in three weeks, and this place has morphed
into a sepia photograph — nothing but white fields
and brown trees, every trunk embraced by its own ghost.

My dogs froze mid-step when the power fizzled,
missing the civilized cacophony of the fridge, the chirp
and beep of everything electronic, not trusting
the depth of dark in which their ancestors thrived.

Weren't they wolves once, who roamed the frozen woods,
hoping for a stray carcass? When did they come to expect
dinner at 7:00 PM under the glow of fluorescent light,
thermometer set to a toasty 70 degrees?

Cocooned in polar fleece, neck wreathed in scarves,
ankles thick as my grandmother's in two pairs of woolen socks,
I stare out at the back deck, dreaming of a steaming cappuccino,
and see the umbrella I neglected to put away at summer's end —

an oasis of color, Tuscan orange, its canopy closed, ribs
holding close to the pole. Winter always dreams of Spring,
but what does Spring dream of?

At the Thrift Shop, Christmas Eve

—Vineyard Haven

Nothing else open and I've an hour to kill
before the ferry arrives, so I go in.

On the radio, Frank and Bing alternately sing.

A woman called Constance greets customers by name as she wrestles
with a stack of puffy winter jackets that keep slipping
from her grip, one by one, asking how Eli's foot is doing
and if, for winter break, Elizabeth is coming home.

Without enthusiasm, a teenaged girl asks if they have any strollers
for twins. Constance says she's been holding one aside, just in case.

I roam around, the way you do when no one knows you,
looking at this and that as relics of my prior lives rise up to catch
my eye like benign ghosts. An exact replica of my Tiny Tears doll,
the one my cousin Randy made blind, poking out her eyes
with two stiff fingers and a twisted smile.

There's a tortoise shell barrette like the one that held back
my schoolgirl hair. Next to it, an ashtray like the one
my mother bought at Lake Placid, featuring a pelican
with an open beak into which she inserted one burning
cigarette after another, before the disease took hold.

And here's a kid's toy chest like the one I struggled with —
assembly instructions on the floor, screws between my lips —
later to become a coffin for stuffed animals with disabilities
and wooden puzzles, missing pieces.

As they prepare to close, an old woman in a man's
double-breasted coat too broad for her shoulders, snags
her walker on a table leg but rights it, regains control.
She admires a magnifying glass with an ivory handle,

yellowed in the grooves, places it in her basket, reconsiders, puts it back. It's Christmas Eve. I want to say I'll pay for whatever she wants but, fearing embarrassment, say nothing.

Constance turns off the radio as the woman makes her way up front and, from a plastic bag, extracts a scrapbook padded with quilted fabric — flips it open to reveal empty slips where photographs are supposed to go.

Hand-stitched, she says. *Made it myself, years ago. Now, give it to someone young enough to fill it.*

Three

The Upside of Numb

How time-efficient
numb is,
all six senses

dispensed with,
all pleasure
a matter

of previous record:
no hunger to humble, no
begged-for taste

of salt on the tongue,
no waiting
for the hand of one

or another, all
that time —
otherwise lost —

now recovered,
and nothing loved
to waste it on.

Beyond Dispute

It wasn't enough: the week's shopping list sutured
to my wrist, an entire room filled with fancy foils
to slap on every birthday and christening gift. Not
enough — the goblet beside your dinner plate, your
favorite wine, perfectly chilled. You wanted it poured.

I'm thinking we could trade in the station wagon
with its simulated oak doors for a used Ducati
or an unlicensed yellow cab or perhaps
a brightly speckled horse. Better yet, let's donate
what we own to some sad museum — I mean, mattresses,

box-springs, sofa and matching love-seat, the two dented
gooseneck lamps — in exchange for a little-known Degas
or an unfinished sketch by Toulouse-Lautrec. Imagine us,
crouched on the floor, the tired walls boasting nothing
but their own shadows and seams, all comforts renounced.

What might we learn? We could do worse than sitting there,
round-backed and without shoes, focused on one small rectangle
or square of indisputable beauty.

Intermittent Hiss

The woman is busy, dusting.
Picking up each piece on the shelves,
dusting beneath it, dusting the thing she's
holding, putting it back, the only sounds
those clicks of matter against matter,
punctuated by the intermittent hiss
of furniture spray.

*Why don't you leave that
and sit down near me?* he says.

She tucks the can under her arm and
with both hands (too heavy for one) lifts
the bust of a crying child, rubs it
across her chest, places it back
in its accustomed spot.

Come. Sit! he says, patting
the couch beside him. The dog
jumps up.

She continues to renew the shine
on everything in sight.

Watching from the corner of his eye,
he still likes the way she moves. He puts down
the paper, comes up behind her, touches the nape
of her neck with one finger.

She flinches, freezes.
He leaves the room.

Later, in bed, the wind forcing itself
through the curtains, making them billow
inward, she says she read somewhere
that if you put candles in the freezer
it takes longer for them to burn.

Fat Crow Above Me

From a rain-stained circle
tunneled in to the rough-shingled
roof, the skylight begins,
in small creaks, to complain.

I crane, look straight up
at the bottoms of two black feet —
three prongs and inches each.
Between them dips the hammock
of a full-bellied crow, round and big
as the cauldron he belongs in.

From below, I see the point
of his blue-black beak as it pecks
at every speck of wet leaf left
from last night's epic squall.

Those legs — wires twisted to tripods
at the ends   imprints thrown across
my chest, the negative of his being
solid as sin on my body beneath,
and him framed, wholly,
by heaven's blue.

Performance Art

When her husband resurfaces
after several hours, she serves him
dinner while he explains — in detail
too absurd not to be true — how he fell
asleep at the hospital, his head resting on a pile
of charts, not one stethoscoped colleague
or nurse having the heart to wake him, no noise
piercing enough to disrupt his slumber —
not the phone in the Medical Records room
she repeatedly caused to ring, nor the beeper she buzzed,
whose battery he says went dead in sympathy and tandem
with the hospital paging system overhead.

How long ago was that? Before he and his lover devised
their private code, before he stopped bringing home
coffee Sunday mornings and blamed the new
medication for making him unable to perform.
Before he began locking his desk, before bottles
of cologne she never bought lined his side
of the medicine cabinet. Before he had his teeth bleached,
changed his part, started wearing pants with pleats
and borrowing his friend's purple convertible,
days when she was away. Tonight on the news, there's
a magician — an illusionist, some say — frozen
by choice inside a solid block of ice. It's Day 3
of this stunt, and the man's pulse has slowed
or, possibly, stopped.

People gawk from the sidewalk and rooftops nearby,
as if this were an amazing feat. Beside her, her husband
snores, exhausted from his round of weekend chores.

Startle Reflex

They've got the choreography down to a science —
her car pulling out as his pulls in. But then, evening,
both skating on the oil slick of silence that spreads
in argument's aftermath.

And now, 3 a.m., slouched at the kitchen counter,
she's making another list of reasons to leave,
balancing each with an excuse not to: the Christmas
cactus she nursed all year about to bloom, kids
coming home from school and who will wrap the gifts
and pick up the uncles arriving from Connecticut?
And then there's that New Year's Eve party they promised
to attend, so not this week or even the next.

From the bedroom where her husband sleeps —
an amorphous sound, the kind that accompanies
the last scene of a bad dream, followed by him
padding quick in bare feet toward the kitchen,
stopping in the doorway.

His body backlit by the light in the hall
as if outlined in chalk, he squints
as he steps in, toes curled against
the coldness of the tiles and, seeing
his wife sitting there, her pen in mid-air,
without thinking, he smiles.

The Sun at Its Widest Point

Over the limit and out of state,
she tailgates the wind
like a church choir riding in
on the sermon's last word

but even at this speed can't escape
what's making her run. Little comfort
that, each time she turns the car around,
it's ten miles further down the road. This

time, she slows to look at what's behind…
the sun, less than an inch above horizon,
trapped in her rear-view mirror, pushing at
the plastic parentheses that contain it. How much

light exists beyond that which she sees,
she can only guess — the height,
the breadth. The heat.

From My Window

From my window upstairs,
I see what the wind was up to
last night, white plastic lawn chairs
tossed around, tipped upside-down,
flung under trees where they kneel
at the trunks like repentant drunks
evicted from the party
of a neighboring friend
to which I listened all night
but did not attend.

Incipient Ice

Their anniversary — the first they both tacitly ignore.
After five days of downpour, the ceiling's begun
to sag. Plastic bowls line the kitchen floor to catch what
the ceiling's too saturated to hold. Placed outside to chill
and then forgotten, the bottle of wine has doubled in size,
enlarged by layer upon layer of sleet that melts, gets rained on
and refreezes. As night crawls toward morning — 4 a.m. —
the doorbell rings, loud and without pause.

From front door to back the woman runs, startled,
holding the hem of her nightgown in the air,
flicking on every light switch as she goes. Nose
to the glass, she peers outside. No one there.
Relief, and then despair. The bell, the bell, the bell.

The sound blares on as the dogs' barks degrade
from menacing to half-hearted, their heads hanging off
the side of the bed now in fatigue, expressions
puzzled, as if questioning their own purpose.

Even after she figures it out, there's nothing she can do.
Rain had run down the roof, seeped into the box outside
that houses the bell and then, tonight, froze —
an invisible guest, his angry thumb stuck to the buzzer.

Who was it? her husband mumbles without interest
as she grabs the pillow from her side of the bed
and pads toward the guest room. *It was for you,*
she says, his head back under the pillow
before she utters the final word.

Through the Funnel of a Loose Fist

Climbing the stairs after the argument,
she sees her husband sideways,
crouched near the bookcase.

With one finger, he hooks the crinkled edge
of a book's binding and tilts it towards him,
rocking it out of place like an old dog's tooth,
adding this one, too, to the tower he's built
without first flipping open the cover
to see who owns it. Words

dissolve like Eucharist on her tongue
as she returns to the kitchen where the wind,
sibilant hours ago through a crack in the caulking,
has now settled down. She fills the kettle
with little more than half an inch
and, while waiting for it to whistle,

transfers the cashews he loves
from the leaf-shaped dish
into a tightly-lidded jar.

Breaking News

You can't imagine how fear drove her pen —
you'd have to see for yourself the 25-page
office phone bill fanned across her desk
beneath the fluorescent lamp, the mint-green
bookkeeping sheet she used, all 30 columns,
to chart the hundreds of calls made from his private line,
how the numbers she scribbled ran down the page
like rodents from the belly of a torpedoed ship.

You'd have to be vigilant, use every trick,
pressing *69 each time you come home
to find out the number of the last incoming
call. You'd have to hold your breath as you
unhook his pants from the bathroom door
to search the pockets for receipts and ticket stubs,
or wait till he's asleep to check his car
in slippered feet and see what's in the glove-box.

And once you discover his lover's number,
you'd have to slip it to a friend, a cop
who offers to run it, and leaves you a message
of just two words. So, that same Friday afternoon

when your husband tells you to call the airline
and confirm his trip to Pompano Beach, you do,
giving the flight numbers, the dates and times
and, when asked for the passenger's name,
from the castanets clicking in your chest you spit out
not his name but the name you've just learned.

And, still, you're stunned to hear it confirmed.

Before the Ground Turns Hard

It's been so long since he's noticed her,
she doubts he'd recall the color

of her eyes, so most of her time she spends
outside, tending the garden, planting annuals

and perennials in voluptuous rows, hibiscus
and witch's broom, lilies and lavender

grown so high and thick they serve as a screen,
blocking his view of her from the house

whenever she's on her knees, then
further blocking it with a birdhouse meant

for barn swallows. Each night in bed, while he
weighs assets against liabilities and schemes

about how to phase out his partner, she turns her back to him
and dreams of running away with the gardener.

The Elastic's Gone Out of the Rubber Band

Spent the morning crouched on the cold basement floor,
disinterring thirty years or more stuffed into cartons
and dented cookie tins. Here's a stack of letters
my ex must have saved but neglected to take —
written by my young hand — held together now
by residue from a slack elastic band.

Under this mumbling fluorescent light, I'm flustered
by the evidence: the unrestrained gush spread thick
across each onion-skinned page, emotions so lush
and eager to be spent they flood the banks, spilling
into the margins with frivolous garlands and curlicues.

How green the trust invested. I'm astounded, so far from
that state of praise for him have I come. I'm thinking now
of Galileo, under house arrest at the end. How, returning
to his early work, he found objects of his own invention
he could no longer comprehend.

Four

After Years of Forced Heat

Is that it? the man at the curb yells to the one coming toward him,
clutching a gooseneck lamp by the neck.

From a window upstairs, the woman watches the men
move in and out of her house, loading her life's odd lot
into the van whose mouth hangs open in an extended yawn.

What she couldn't sell, she keeps — furniture with infirmities,
inherited and worthless when she got it: a wobbly desk chair,
its leg-length discrepancy chronic; that coffee table her sister-in-law
spilled nail polish on, the red blot seeping under the finish

in a clot that cannot be dissolved. From one bedroom to the next,
stopped by doors intended to connect but long stuck shut,
she uses her hip to undo them, walking through each room

where someone she loved has lived, noticing how things she kept
pressed against walls have left their mark, the outlines so distinct
a stranger could place each piece back into its habitual spot.

Next time she'll keep all the furniture in the middle of the room.

Picking up a small ball of dust and pocketing it, she walks out
the front door as once she came in, closing but not locking it.

Floored

I'm speeding through Summit where, this afternoon,
the stench from the pharmaceutical plant
is overruled by Star Gazer lilies, tilting toward me
from the passenger seat, cocooned
in a pink paper cone. I'm driving

too fast, whole foot on the gas,
to the house of the woman he left me for,
the woman who, to this day, he insists
he's never met. My tires squeal

as they scrape her curb. The back bumper
of his brown sedan protrudes
from her one-car garage like a hamburger
too big for the bun. How dare he

send me flowers, assume I'll accept them,
this second Sunday in May? How obscene,
this ostentatious display: a week's worth
of groceries we could well use and too big
by half for any vase I own.

Propelled, I march up the flagstone path,
step onto the gray painted porch and draw
a quick breath, pressing the bell and turning
to run as the lilies hit the floor, hard.

Let her be the one who comes to the door.
Let her read the words he wrote, let her see
how he signed the card.

Mistress

He uses her sparingly,
between his divorces,
like Europeans use sorbet
to cleanse the palate
between courses.

Waves and Light

—For my brother

I.   one month into the coma   one kidney's failed
one lung is filled   one doctor said
pneumonia while the others refer to
a little problem we've got going on in the lungs
we sit and discuss   your functions without you
like a friendship where one side spills their guts
and the other remains mute   in the ICU waiting room
other lives intrude   a young man and his
pregnant wife share a cheeseburger   taking one bite each
passing it back and forth on a soggy paper plate a family
with two boys named Kyle   huddles near
the fake ficus tree   gum wrappers stuck
in the decorative mulch   in a dim corner by
the magazines a white-haired woman cries
without urgency in a blue vinyl chair   turns
around and around a tissue in her hand   looking
for a surface she hasn't used   six full coffee cups
still issuing steam   abandoned on a table
someone turns on the TV to a show about
river dolphins the narrator says how their eyes
have almost disappeared and now   they must
navigate by sound alone   the reception's poor the picture
mostly grey fuzz but color   every now
and then appears tomorrow being   your birthday
a daughter will bring earphones   your wife
Beethoven's 9th   we watch your closed lids
for signs as the orchestra plays for you   alone
and the night nurse   amends your age on the chart
arching her arms   across the breadth
of your motorized bed   as it undulates on   and on
in one   slow   arduous   wave

II.   In a coma just shy of a year, my brother
        opens his eyes and tells me where he was.

        The door, he says, was too heavy to budge
        but somehow, he managed to slip in, amazed
        to find he'd arrived in German Heaven.
        Who knew, each nation has its own?

        Overwhelmed by light (as blinding, he says,
        as Ebbets Field at night), the glow
        distorted every dimension, making it hard
        to distinguish depth from height, but dead
        center he saw an old man who commanded
        all attention with his battlefield skin,
        remnants of a black morning-coat hanging
        bat-like from his shoulders in broad strips,
        a wand in one bone-thin hand.

        Moving his arms in sweeping arcs,
        pausing but never stopping, his exhaustion
        expressed in periodic grunts, sweat glazing
        the trenches of his face — but the light, the light!

        In spite of the hostile audience (scorched angels
        with burnt wings, angry, scolding) the man
        never lost focus, even as the angels marched
        backwards, away, a forest of burnt trunks…

        The night nurse interrupts, disconnects
        the morphine drip, says my brother
        will be hooked up again by her replacement
        on the graveyard shift. As she leaves,
        he jabs repeatedly at my sleeve, says in a voice
        desperate to finish and desperately thin:

        *and that man   was Beethoven
        and all the light   came   from him.*

Absent Without Leave

He's sorry for being gone so long
but he was summoned urgently
to Tennessee. This, my brother tells me
as I mix a packet of blue dye into the applesauce
the nurse urges me to feed him.

Most of the way, he says he rode the train
but jumped off to walk the last 900 miles,
trying to lose whoever was following him, probably
some gumshoe from the FBI. Only a handful
of citizens are ever admitted to this society (he
shouldn't even be telling me this). Of course,
in a secret pocket sewn into his coat he carried
the wooden balls which only he
knows how to fit into the square sockets
the society keeps under lock and key, along with
their exploding flowers and collapsing rubber knives.
His appearance was to be the main event, of course,
but then the storm hit — that tornado
I might have read about that sent cows
whirling through the air like black-and-white pinwheels…

Needless to say, the storm derailed his plans
and forced him to cut his trip short. But why
is this applesauce blue and his arm taped to a board,
and how does he know the IV isn't truth serum
and the nurse complicit, and if I were a good sister
I'd put a spoonful of that disgusting stuff
in my own mouth first, and did anyone
at least miss him when he was gone
for so long, gone and sailing almost free
on a train of thought
to, of all the places
he'd never want to be,
Tennessee?

All Holy

Raised in a home where saving
was the only grace and faith a beast
to be skewered and stuffed, I find myself
alone at the deep end of the self-help aisle,
facing a plethora of Bibles.

How to proceed, for those with no previous footing
in faith? How to choose, when most versions
of the Lord's words come blister-wrapped —
no peeking allowed.

Some kind of sampler would be nice,
like the flooring chips you can take
from the home improvement store
and live with for a while before you buy…

I think I'll pick this one, the smallest of the lot
that will fit easily in pocket or purse — and I shall
carry it with me and move my lips as I read, like
that woman with swollen feet and a 4-footed cane

who rides the #60 from Newark to Bloomfield
every day, mumbling her rosary with eyes closed
until the driver pulls up to the Job Haines Old Age Home
and someone taps her on the shoulder, someone
helps her off the bus.

Absolution on the Ferry

A bulky baby on the boat's top deck
squats to squeeze the nose
of a chocolate Lab,

then suddenly raises a fist,
emitting a high-pitched squeal,
punching the dog roundly
on the snout.

The dog snarls, growls, moves
only his eyes. The mother grabs
for her child while three guys
passing by jump to defend the dog.

Both hands dug in to his shiny coat,
the baby grunts as the mother yanks her
by the feet. The harder the mother pulls,

the harder the baby holds, her body
Jacob's ladder between immovable poles.
Uncertainty freezes time. No one here knows

how this opus will end. Nothing gives —
until, as if synchronized, the foghorn bleats
and the baby screams and the stricken dog,

an inch from the baby's face, gives
one long sacramental lick —
and the baby, forgiven, cries.

Richer for Its Absence

I kept meaning to replace it, fill the square
where one piece of slate somehow disappeared
from the patio last fall. Before I knew it, though,
a crowd of leaves gathered, acting as attorneys
for its defense, and I left the emptiness alone.

Come winter, the space filled with rain and froze,
broken twigs skating the length of it till they banked
in mounds of snow. And now in May, as five kinds
of flowering trees dispense their petals like rations
to the poor, the breeze sweeps clean the stone floor,

deposits a host of pink and white blooms (two, three
inches deep) into that vacant square — and only there! —
a coffer with no lid, storing all the seasons' softest offerings,
the slabs that surround it now greyer, duller, begging
for any hint of color.

Prayer

deargod dear God dear
barking dog in the neighbor's yard
dear staked birch staccato heart dear
rabid raccoon trapped between ceiling and roof all religions
are true they all my son swears say
the same thing in different ways so does it
matter what I call you should I say Lord
or god or mother or wind dear dead
brown leaf holding to the window screen
like a moth should I
roll back the rug so my knees bare
against the hardwood floor
hurt more am I saying this right I mean
I've seen the old women in black shawls
at the shrine crawling in the heat
leaving pale pink dots on the concrete
then larger spots cardinal red
the path leading to the marble steps and black-robed priests
who take their arms and raise them to their feet
but blind faith is Greek to me
so what's the pecking order
the etiquette here must an agnostic daughter
pray harder than a baptized son   an old friend born
again with one hand on my head issues commands in a tone
certain of being heard a list of things for You to do
on my behalf saying
And, Lord, make her prosper in every way
when my request was just
to let my brother live   another day

Non-Stop Scarlet

Sounds less like a plant than a popular harlot,

but for nine bucks I take home from Maloney's Nursery
and place on my patio table this *Non-Stop Scarlet
Tuberous Begonia* whose petals — ruffled and red
as the Rockettes' raised skirts — display themselves
in brazen layers atop their hairy stems.

Weeks later, after wind has swept away
the sapped blooms, a new improved version appears —
less dense, the petals no longer ruffled but smooth,
the center of each flower pure yellow now
as if, overnight, filled with light.

How did Scarlet re-invent herself so soon? How quickly
she's raced through the slow-paced stages of my life,
catching up in just a few short weeks to my decades spent
in search of my self: learning to shed her more frivolous frills
and reveal, instead, what's at the core.

Settling

Lately
even her nightmares are mild:
someone's birthday forgotten,
a shirt she burned with a too-hot iron.

Fantasies as well
have lost their edge and settled
like a jumper crawling back in from the ledge: last night
she pictured herself fevered,

and then a man
standing near her bed, his hand
pressed to her forehead,
asking how she felt.

Shutter

I still remember the roughness of the warped
wooden door as I tried to wrestle it closed, the loose
hinge that threw it off-kilter so the bottom scraped
against the cement floor. I remember dropping

the hook into the rusted eye that kept it shut
while I took off my bathing suit to shower before
going in to the boarding house where old men
came to spend a week at the beach and left
combs with missing teeth in the rented rooms.

I can still feel sand in the soap, from guests
who went before me, how the grains
scratched and grated a 6-year-old's skin,
can smell the mildew that formed in the corners
despite the large opening left above the door
to allow the salt air in, but I remember, as well,

the scent of honeysuckle sweltering sweet
in the ripples of summer heat, the irritated hum
of bees that circled and invaded it and, from the blue
shuttered house a few feet away, the smell of brisket

and boiled potatoes drifting from the kitchen
where my grandmother and aunt manned
the sink and the stove, placing platters
on the sticky oilcloth where
the man with no neck ate pie.

I can still see myself naked as a skinned peach,
reaching for the towel draped over the door,
how I turned toward the window at the camera's click
and caught my father's startled face. How quickly
he ducked and the curtains, stiff with starch, fell back
into place, as if they'd never been touched.

Praise for the Corpse Flower

Bless the *Amorphophallus Titanum* with its one colossal shoot,
   the ten-foot-tall 'corpse flower' whose horrid smell
   mimics the rotting carrion above which it blooms.

Should we not praise the flower, despite its perfume?

Some applause, then, for the rabid dog, the lapsed priest,
   the unconvicted guilty, freed on their own recognizance.

Let's extol the barker, the telemarketer, the bigot, the boil,
   the swollen splinter dug deep, reddening your thumb.

One cheer each for the atheist and agnostic, for the scientist
   studying lunar rocks — ungodly hours, at 100 watts — and

how about the leagues of blue-haired thieves
   whose purses bulge with sugar packets, napkins, salt?

Kudos for recidivists like the roach and the self-obsessed talk show host.

 Salvos for the pervert, the pimp, the centerfold.

 A little hymn, too, for the also-rans: the torn ligament, the ruptured
   spleen, the dented can.

No confetti for the wet match, the little toe, the perpetually lesser than? I say,

   praise every crumb that falls, forever lost between cushions
     of the couch. Recognize the spent life. The long haul. Acclaim
     both sides of the hyphenated wife (battered- and -beater both),
     all jack-knifed, flailing, into the same free fall.

Praise the least of us, praise us all.

Five

Request Denied

At the end, no one showed but us:

distant daughter, twice-disowned son
and Wife #6, cracking gum, practicing
your signature on the last withdrawal slip.
Who else did you think would come?
From what source a guest list drawn, a crowd

to rally as you sank, yacht-sails dragged through
water you fouled? Perhaps a priest to anoint
you, proud atheist, on your way down? Maybe
Wife #4, bearing a basket of fruit and the knife
she tried to stab you with? Or would you prefer
to take the 5th?

Which of your siblings, long deleted from
your mailing list, did you expect to make the trip,
to cough up six bucks for gas, plus tolls? And which
of us (your two children, known) owed you so much
as an hour of our grown-up time, you who never
held a hand or gave a dime?

Hard to admit — country-club Communist
short-tipping your caddy, sweet-timing
saccharine sugar daddy, buttering your way
in and out of wedding rings (more than enough
for one entire hand). In the end, even you
wanted tears and a 6-piece band.

How poorly you planned.

On This Filthy February Morning

As I lurk on the back porch
filled with distressed furniture
from deceased aunts,
waves of sleet smack
against the crust of old snow
in my backyard
and everyone else's.

Three cacti
received as a gift
from someone
not enough of a friend
to come empty-handed
cringe in a corner
like ugly triplets
at the school dance.

I seldom remember
to water them.

In spite of which this morning,
extruded from thorny points
at the border of each leaf —

delicate buds, tentative and tight —
like girls in their first stiff bras,
preening toward the day's meager
yet magnificent measure of light.

That Date

You remember the lamb and mashed potatoes you ate
that night, how you fell asleep before the news
only to have the phone wake you at 5:00 A.M. — the numbers
big and red on the digital clock, saying "Bad,"

and the doctor's voice, flat, uttering the one word
that stopped the others — dead — and how you rocked
in her flowered chair, both arms wrapped tight
around your legs, how you chose not to wake the kids,

stalling until dawn, listening to your husband make long-distance calls,
an endless recitation of events leading up to and including
her last breath. Sure, you would have flown a single-engine plane
blindfolded, through a blizzard, you would have ripped from its socket

your one good arm and given it to her, whole — but what, really, did you do?
You groped your way through the narrow hall like any other gutted soul.
Perhaps you slept less, maybe wept a little more, but nothing sets
this death apart, now, does it? How many mothers, before yours, have died?

You remember sinking, your body dropping like a plumb line from the top
of the Empire State Building onto the quilt, thinking things will never, you
will never, life will never… yet here it is, that date again on the calendar's page,
not in bold print but with the same amount of ink allotted any other.

Unbareable Heat

Three days without power in triple-digit heat
drives the town's thirsty elders to this corner
where the ice cream shop and coffee bar meet.
The line of sweating patrons, two abreast,
stretches half way down the street.

I undo two, then three of the buttons
on my linen shirt, hesitate to roll up the long sleeves,
fearing the wrinkles may never come out. I'm debating
whether to fold up the cuffs of my thick but slenderizing
black pants when I notice the woman standing next to me.

More ancient than old, she sports a pair
of short shorts and a drooping halter top.
From both her knees and thighs, richly varicosed
skin drapes like bunting from firehouse windows.

My first thought — which I'm loathe to admit — is:
Kill me if I ever look like that. Which quickly yields
to a hot blush of shame and then, an overwhelming
sense of envy — for her defiance of fashion tips
for women over 90, her vanity-be-damned belief
in comfort over personal conceit. Just then

she leans toward me to offer a stick of gum and says:
*Poor thing — look at you, all bundled up. You must've come
from someplace cold.*

Big Happy

Remember the kind of love
where you're so insane with wonder,
you want to witness every move,
listen to every utterance from profound
to mundane, every hiccup that issues
from the beloved's lips? You want to slip

like a pebble into his pocket
and be swept along wherever he goes
or be the tortoise shell clip that holds
her hair on top of her head all day
to survey her world from there,
not so much to eavesdrop
as to know, to know everything —

what makes her laugh, what
makes him cry — when every skipped
beat causes your heart to seize
and lungs to pause mid-breath
for fear of missing one syllable,
how your existence is pinned

to the next point of contact
and, once there, you can never
get enough. You want to live
like Lambert the cat — twice as wide
as his doctor recommends — who resides
at Alley's General Store, surprising

every customer who bends to grab a sack
of flour from the bottom shelf and pulls
back in dread when something moves:

it's Lambert the cat, asleep, his big happy head
tucked inside a torn bag of cat food, grateful
to live in the place where his soul is fed.

Peekskill Possibilities

I knew   or thought I knew   my father
was in prison when my brother was born
radical they said   whispers from relatives
in the other room   union organizer
Singer sewing machines   baseball bats and bricks
and something about Paul Robeson   a blacklist and
a concert he was giving   in Peekskill New York
and my mother and father there   together
faced with maniacs smashing windows   slashing tires
and our old brown Pontiac with the running board
rocked back and forth   rowdy crowds of anti-Communists
come to disrupt   and my mother's glasses cracked to bits
and the only aunt my father ever liked was
supposed to be Red although   no one really spoke of it
and once she said Ginger Rogers was a homosexual
and my cousin Joni and I howled   behind her back
because Ginger Rogers was after all   a *girl*
and now in bed   one a.m.   I catch
the tail end of a documentary
about Robeson's life and I'm forcing
myself to stay awake because I know he
was at Peekskill   with Pete Seeger
who stayed at my grandmother's boarding house
once (without the Weavers) for a week
and maybe they'll show the riot
and somewhere there'll be proof of how
the police stood by with arms folded
across their wide blue chests
and allowed the mayhem to ensue   and if
I can keep   my eyes open maybe
in the middle of the crowd
halfway up or down   the hill

near the ridge of serrated pines
I'll see my mother
and my father   young
if the rumors were true
imagine   the two of them   together
in the same frame
maybe he'll throw his arm around
her shoulder as they duck their heads
maybe he'll brush some glass
from the bridge of her nose
reach out to grab her arm
pull her towards him
maybe in the face of such danger
surrounded by chaos and comrades and
the cause that he loved
maybe
he loved her too   my
mother   that day.

Ellipsis

In the mall parking lot, behind the Iranian salesman
and me, a wedding-sized tent housing his wealth —
a thousand Persian carpets, guarded by armed men
at either side of the entrance.

Although I insist I don't intend to buy, in slow English
he describes how the carpets were made, before the age
of synthetics and dyes — each worker an artisan
with a keen eye, using pistachios for green, walnut meats
for brown, henna for rust, rose petals rubbed against
the grain to obtain a deep blood red. Out of the blue,
he asks if I like poetry and starts reciting Hafiz, by heart —
first in Farsi, to "feel the texture" on his tongue, and then
in verses I had long loved and memorized, years ago.
Come back later, he says, *after I close.*

I must have appeared an easy mark, a thin line
of pale white skin where, until today,
my wedding band was parked.

On the drive home, in that uncertain light
when layers of shadow duel at dusk, a stream
of deer emerges from the woods, forcing me
to pause as they cut across my path
with no introduction, no foreseeable aftermath.

Boilerplate

Why do people bother getting married anymore,
given the odds? Are they wedded to tradition
like a bulldog to a stick — statistics be damned —
or is it their belief (brave or naïve) that love
can conquer all but the common cold?

Once, I was convinced if you poured every cell
of yourself into it, love would return in kind.
Years, feeding silver into the slot machine,
pulling the lever again and again with equal measures
of hope until my wealth was spent. Of course, you
who've been there know: soon as I left,
another woman slid in to my still-warm seat
and reaped what I was owed.

Still, if I were young and it were spring
in Paris or Rome, and from his chromed-up bike
a man called my name, his fist curled loose
on the rubber grip, a space behind him saved for me
and a bouquet of daisies tied to the spit-shined shaft,
wouldn't I go?

Day of Atonement

You can be brushing your teeth or pairing socks
or rushing down a side street to catch a bus
when the thought hits: there's nothing

in your mundane life to atone for — no juicy sins,
no new lover stashed at some mildewed motel, no
bundle of cash in a locked metal box. Not you: you've

played by the rules, bitten your tongue, done your job.
Next thing you know, you're staring into a jewelry store

someone else just robbed.

Even though the alarm's been tripped
and, peripherally, you can see the spinning red lights
and hear the sirens drawing near, you suck in

your bottom lip and, reaching through glass
the previous looter broke, you scoop up what's left —
a thin gold chain, a topaz ring propped on a black velvet

swatch — whatever you can steal, however much you feel
entitled to, you pluck from the glittering spread, clutch it

to your felon's breast, and you're alive, and you run.

Gifts from a Crow

I fed the crow
until the food ran out,
then fed him parts
of my heart.

When I fed the crow
the wounded part,
he brought me
a strip of gauze.

I fed the crow
the angry part
and he brought me
a broken razor blade.

When I fed the crow
the giving part —
silver sequins
scattered at my door!

I fed the crow
the motherly part
and he brought me
a feather from a baby bird,
tipped by the fuzzy down
of the feather that
preceded it.

When I fed the crow
the trusting part,
he brought me
twigs pulled from his nest.

I fed the crow
the selfish part.
That day he
brought me
nothing.

When I fed the crow
the stubborn part,
he brought me
the same thing
as the day before.

I fed the crow
the jealous part
and he brought me
a newborn, pink and dead,
eyes never opened, so young
I couldn't tell
what it was.

When I fed the crow
the one part left — bright red,
a swollen sliver of joy — he nudged it,

puffed up his chest and left it
where it lay, then rose and cawed
and cawed, crowing
as he flew away.

Vanishing Point at the Inlet

I park beneath the only tree, a scarred sycamore
with knuckled limbs stretching toward
the water where inlet opens to ocean.

This is my summer office. Here, no traffic
but grackles and crows. A decent breeze.
An old boat that bobbles beyond the sea grass.

Every so often, another curious tourist
noses his car into this half-hidden cove,
pops out, takes a picture and departs.

And every afternoon I sit, windows down,
reading a book and, between chapters, contemplate
the shingle fixed with one rusty nail to the tree's trunk.
I feel an affinity — both sign and me
weathered to anonymity.

Who came to this unnamed spit of land, hammer
in hand, to nail the shingle there (or did they use a rock)?
What message to convey? *No trespassing? Will you marry me?*
How many storms before the words washed away?

And who am I — years without a tongue — to be the one
to give it voice? Each day of summer I've wondered: why
me, why did I happen to find this particular tree with its
blank sign begging for something to profess?

I grab my permanent marker, get out of the car
and, in firm strokes, print the word:

Yes.

About the Author

Susan Berlin's poems have appeared in *Alaska Quarterly, Asheville Poetry Review, Atlanta Review, Cape Cod Poetry Review, Georgetown Review, Harvard Review, Iodine Poetry Review, JMWW Quarterly, Mudfish, Naugatuck River Review, New Millennium Writings, Oberon, Ploughshares* and *South Road,* among others. Twice a finalist for the National Poetry Series and a multiple Pushcart Prize nominee, she was awarded First Prize in the Galway Kinnell Poetry Contest by the Rhode Island Council on the Arts and has received an International Publication Prize as well as an International Merit Award from *Atlanta Review*. She lives in Yarmouth Port, MA.

Glass Lyre Press

exceptional works to replenish the spirit

Glass Lyre Press is an independent literary publisher interested in technically accomplished, stylistically distinct, and original work. Glass Lyre seeks diverse writers that possess a dynamic aesthetic and an ability to emotionally and intellectually engage a wide audience of readers.

Glass Lyre's vision is to connect the world through language and art. We hope to expand the scope of poetry and short fiction for the general reader through exceptionally well-written books, which evoke emotion, provide insight, and resonate with the human spirit.

Poetry Collections
Poetry Chapbooks
Select Short & Flash Fiction
Anthologies

www.GlassLyrePress.com

www.ingramcontent.com/pod-product-compliance
Lightning Source LLC
Chambersburg PA
CBHW021157080526
44588CB00008B/375